DERIVING

Jennifer Bowering Delisle

DERIVING

UNIVERSITY *of* ALBERTA PRESS

Published by

University of Alberta Press
1-16 Rutherford Library South
11204 89 Avenue NW
Edmonton, Alberta, Canada   T6G 2J4
uap.ualberta.ca

LIBRARY AND ARCHIVES CANADA
CATALOGUING IN PUBLICATION

Title: Deriving / Jennifer Bowering
    Delisle.
Names: Delisle, Jennifer Bowering, 1979–
    author.
Description: Poems.
Identifiers:
    Canadiana (print) 20200372343 |
    Canadiana (ebook) 2020037236X |
    ISBN 9781772125474 (softcover) |
    ISBN 9781772125641 (PDF)
Classification: LCC PS8607.E4844 D47
    2021 | DDC C811/.6—dc23

First edition, first printing, 2021.
First printed and bound in Canada by
Houghton Boston Printers, Saskatoon,
Saskatchewan.
Editing and proofreading by
Jannie Edwards.

A volume in the Robert Kroetsch Series.

University of Alberta Press is committed
to protecting our natural environment.
As part of our efforts, this book is printed
on Enviro Paper: it contains 100% post-
consumer recycled fibres and is acid- and
chlorine-free.

University of Alberta Press gratefully
acknowledges the support received
for its publishing program from the
Government of Canada, the Canada
Council for the Arts, and the
Government of Alberta through the
Alberta Media Fund.

Canadä | Canada Council for the Arts | Conseil des Arts du Canada

Alberta Government

For Kenton,
Malcolm, and Coralie

deriving

from Old French deriver, to pour out

from Latin derivare, to lead water from its source

from Latin de rivus, from the stream

CONTENTS

ETYMOLOGY

Descartes thought worms birthed spontaneous
in soil and heat. Sudden maggots in rotting flesh
were proof of God. Until Francesco Redi
placed meat in sealed and open flasks,
watched worms devour skinned frogs.

Entomology: from entomos, meaning cut,
      cut up. *The barbarous sound*
                    terrify'd me
said naturalist Charles Bonnet, preferring *insectology*
for his caterpillar breath, for cleaving
the hydra's head
             watching it grow back.
For his portion of the effort
to catalogue all Earth's creatures.
Etymology: from etumos, meaning true.

You can tell a carnivore
by the contents of the belly.
                 English
shares the words for meat with French
      (beef/boeuf, pork/porc)
but the words for animals with German
      (cow/kuh, swine/schwein).
This a story of the Norman conquest
of who ate the meat and who farmed it,
just as other words tell other stories
of things catalogued
            consumed—banana, curry
of shores landed on and flagged, specimens
pinned in curiosity cabinets, and larger creatures

ogled in menageries.

            Kangaroo.

                 Orangutan.

English is formed by deriving
and compounding,
onomatopoeia,
and loanwords,
a term that falsely suggests
we give them back.

And if we could, give them back
      if we would
it would be as cut, not as truth. Not
as animal, alive and growing, but as meat
that's been in our mouths.

WATER IN A
BLUE GLASS

CARIBOU

When you first brought me home to meet your dad,
you led me through the snow, through the gate,
to the caribou he raised.
Cloud of breath and hoof, eyes like burrows.
You asked what "flavour" I was—
a way of asking ethnicity
without ugly words, with the levity
of candy, hint of tongue
for the young first falling in love.
Back then, these were light questions
for light skin. There were no stakes, no scrip,
nothing to prove. We fed the caribou
tendrils of moss they ate like candy
and they kicked at the ground, buried
their snouts. Snow-shoveller—qalipu

the Mi'kmaq word that French and English morphed.
Just Canadian, I said.
I was a guest here, but already at home,
snow skin on your lips.
You said you were a mix of everything, like a roll
of lifesavers. You did not say
Métis. Back then,

crunching through the drifts,
that we called them caribou in Canada
made me proud. I thought reindeer
named for reins around muzzles,
for tether, for dash away,
whistle and down.
Caribou was Strong and Free
despite this fence around us.

2

But reindeer is from Saami, raingo.
Just as there are other names
in Cree, Gwich'in, Inuktitut
I had never heard, and other histories
I did not understand. Just as
there were always stakes
stuck in snow, for all of us,
always histories distorted or denied.

You tell me that back then
you were still finding words
for who you are, amidst the noise—
murmurs of the ones who had to pass
and echoes of your grandma spitting
I didn't marry an Indian.
There are no Indians in this family

and I'm still finding words
for everything I'll never understand.

SEEDS

There'd been tales of blood from older girls,
and rumours: he puts it *where?*
My report is on seeds, Hannah whispered in the library,
so I can get the S encyclopedia. We discovered
dirty words we'd not heard before:
gamete, blastocyst.
Flipped the page when teacher passed.

Essential for the propagation of a species. The male's erect penis is
inserted into the female's vagina. Rhythmic thrusting results in the
male ejaculation of semen, which contains sperm, into the vagina.

Babies came from sleeping together. Simply
put Ken with Barbie in the bed, and then
a scrunchee beneath her dress. But we knew
that Ken was incomplete in more than elbow joints.
Something we were missing. Laughing
with the sitcom track, then Mom asking
quietly as she tucked me in,
did you understand what you were laughing at?

The sperm travels into the fallopian tubes or uterus and fertilizes the
ovum. The fertilized ovum produces a zygote, which develops into
an offspring.

Still, the Britannica could not explain
all the ways that bodies fit together
like seed and husk, leaf and water. Caress of word
touch of look, shared breath, beads of
progesterone and vials of gonadotropin, holding
a cup of your sperm beneath my coat
to keep it warm.

Certain species also reproduce by nonsexual means; sea anemones
and marine worms, for example, bud off parts of their bodies in
certain seasons.

In the library we snickered *ew* when we knew
we should, pictured ourselves women
with women's hips and Barbie breasts. Babies
growing beneath our dresses. Now we know,
we thought. Tried not to think
about the way we were made, but imagined
a boy's thing between our thighs
and everything our futures held.

THE WAY WE STAND

Hawk, did you see it?

I see highway, cloud, sometimes cows,
roadkill like a wine-spilled coat.
He sees plumage within blur, molt
on wingspan of moth. You can tell cormorants
by the way they stand, he says,
their legs so far back.

He always cheers for the animals,
rampaging shark, reanimated dinosaur.
He has rubbed the bums of newborn rats
to simulate a mother's licking,
as a child he shared his ice cream with his dog.

Yet one evening on our scrap of wild
he blocks me, turns me to the door,
gently scoops the empty feather frock
beak and bone abandoned in the grass
to lay it down to leaf-lined rest. It is an act of love
to spare me, who does not grieve, from the guts,
the glimpse of death. An act of love
to offer this magpie's trace
the gentleness of his hands.

So now I squint into the sun,
wondering what wings make that shadow
unfurling from the telephone pole.
You can spot me by my stance,
the direction I lean.

INSTINCT

My Psych 101 prof taught that love is only reproductive instinct.
Most took notes. A few protested, in the classroom or our heads,
feeling sorry for his wife. I was not so primal.
We were the creatures painting ceilings
with our plans, naked on the floor. Careers, house, someday
a child. The distance sweet for the view it offered,
like stepping back in a gallery.

Years later, this wanting is not art but thirst.
A baboon in a Polish zoo adopts a chick meant for her dinner.
A penguin treks to the coldest place on Earth to lay her egg
and put her hopes upon her partner's feet. I preen and call, cry
when the blood comes, cry when the sitcom wife conceives.
My territory is envy and fear. I mark it by peeing
on ovulation predictor strips.

The penguins come here, far from the sea, because the ice
is solid for the colony. The one whose chick has died
will try to steal the baby of another, her grief blinding
off the snow. She has trekked 70 miles to bring her baby food.
It's not known how she finds her way.

When they tell us the baby inside me has died
we grasp each other as if drowning. It's a leading cause of divorce
but we have grown our marriage like gills.
We'll huddle beneath our grief and watch *Game of Thrones*.
We've had enough statistics.

The penguin finds her mate amongst the squawking thousands
by his unique call. Somehow she hears him in the noise.
And I still know he was wrong—Professor Whatshisname—about love.
It is not a sneeze or suckle, not a pupil widening in the dark.
But he was right about the soma and the axon,
the number and names of lobes of the brain.
We have lived for thousands of years.

REASONS

If you are trying too hard. If you expect it. If you mark time in months without names. If you're stressed. If your wanting is not the right kind of wanting, not patient, not saintly. Void of grace. Crone clawed, lurking. If you have a negative attitude or outlook. Sulphur eggs, green and grainy, crumbling in their dessicated tubes. If you can't just relax. If your sex is duty, punch in hips, austere choreography. If you planned it and could see it. If you did not see it well enough. If the ticking is not clock but bomb, and everywhere bellies point like canons. If you are grieving. If you forgot that at this time of year the cherry blossoms burst their limbs, brash with life, a million pink-tinged follicles. If there's trash in the hedge, a fly in the dark, a moon in the sky, if you feel like you have lost yourself—if you have

FEBRUARY IN VANCOUVER

My eyes are blurred with sleep when the corner's lint
darts across tile. Silverfish
surfacing from drains, or falling from fan to tub's pink gleam.

Rain without rhythm—the roof is three floors up.
Just spray of tires, steps of unknown neighbours on my head
(garbage leaker, movie blaster, lighter in the lint trap prick).
I study weight of cloud, scavenging for blue.
I bet you don't miss prairie winters, they say
and I can't explain, the sun,

the *sun*

how I'd trade any winter rain for the colour
of the open sky, the trick of light as blue
enveloping the earth, deepened by the cold
and filling as bread.

Silverfish thrive in this humid climate
and the internet says they
can live a year without food.

EMBRYOPATHOLOGY REPORT

Blighted ovum at 8 weeks.

Blight: potatoes corked with fungus,

rotten in the fields. This is my child.

Products of conception: placental villi present. Specimen

consists of pale fragments of deciduas and mucus thin

skim of life holding a dream of cells, erupting tooth,

scraped knee. Hair wet from the bath. Chorion submitted for

parting. Pale fragments of love.

Amnion not grossly differentiated degenerating decidua normal

male karyotype It was a boy It was a boy It was

a smear of DNA in my belly, codes that leave

a trace of a child like fingerprints

low on the wall.

GIFTS

I.

You told me you sat in the bathtub
    and wrote,
         and wrote.
I took these words as offering,
gift. Though daughters now
encircle you, tutu-ed in rose,
you too once knew the pink
of blood on tile.

Frida Kahlo painted herself
naked on a bed.
Snail, orchid, machine,
fetus
    floating red, tied with umbilical bows.
Pubic hair matted with blood.

This too, a gift.
Pain like a plate of food, a flower
severed from its root.

II.

Discharged from loss—
Doff the gown but keep
the privacy,
its comfortable ignorance.

Scrape the matter
from my tongue.

The unborn remain
in my throat.

III.

Frida said she did self-portraits
because she was so often alone.

IV.

Careless happiness
slung over their shoulders,
bumping heads down the bus aisle.
I say I wouldn't wish this loss
on anyone,
and yet I would.

I want to sit in your tub,
I want to lie with Frida
in her bloody bed
in Henry Ford Hospital, 1932,
smokestacks trimming the world.

v.

I want to fill my ears with the wailing
of her red paint.

On her deathbed Frida wrote,
I hope the exit is joyful
and I hope never to return.

But they say that at the crematorium
the blast of heat made her sit up again,
her hair ablaze.

VI.

André Breton once called Frida
a ribbon around a bomb.
I will take her gift.
Put my ear to it and shake.
Take comfort in the deafening.

GRAVITY

from Latin gravis, for weight. And before cannonballs and apples
dropped from towers, it also meant solemnity, burden. Heavy
already metaphor when Earth was not yet round.

I had to drop an egg from the school roof. Cotton cradles,
elastic nets, parachutes of plastic—I don't recall what I made,
or what was taught of velocity or force. I learned
gravity's certainty. The different ways things break.

You learned these lessons other ways. Mass and impact,
oscillation of loss. The earth ellipses in the dark.
The moon is falling like the apple.

Sometimes yokes are flecked with blood.
We know gravitas not gravid, we know hollows lead weights make
on ground. And we know the pull of bodies broken and celestial.
Lie with me, place your face between my shoulder blades
and I'll hold your head in my sling of skin. I learned

build a nest the best you can, hold your breath as it falls.

KNOW THE WAY

The walk out of the clinic and through the building back to the car is long.
I put my sunglasses on in the elevator.
There are people in the hallways. There is a bench and a plant.
I will walk around them.
There is a parking lot to cross, tarmac desert and sun too bright, too hot
for the winter in my belly.

You are beside me. We walk together
squinting into the white light, even through our shades. All those windshields.
I wonder if you can drive.

We have been here before.
Here, in a different parking lot. Then it was fall
and the leaves were yellow and stuck to our shoes and the words stuck
in our ears.
There is no heartbeat. There is nothing there.
And our legs still moved, and we walked to the car.

Later you will say, I did not think it would happen again.
You will say, I did not think we'd be so unlucky.

Now our steps clap across the pavement. They do not sound different.
And the sun is in my eyes and my eyes are red as the sun,
hidden behind my shades.
I walk as if the world is flat.
The car will be just where we left it, halfway down this row.
We will reach it.
Our bodies know the way.

VANCOUVER

I know it's raining by the hunch
of people on the street below,
as if they are grieving.

The weather's not coincidence—
it always rains, there's always loss
running down my windows.

But you and I are wringing out our bodies,
taking them in from the elements.
We will lay down towels in the porch
and drip until we're dry.

We'll squint and blink into the light
spread blankets on the lawn, and later,
aloe on each other's pink shoulders.

We are leaving this city
leaving loss like an address
running from gods and pressure systems

leaving loss like a forecast
knowing everywhere has sky
but in this city we have seen
a thousand ways to block the sun.
Today they say the hazy skies
are from Russian fires.

ANEMOCHORY

Stop, here, we shout. Right here.
As if in a taxi.

But this is anemochory:
We are seeds on a gale
clutching air with pale pappus fingers.
We are hooked burrs clinging
to the fur of animals.

Once, we waited to be set down
and grow where we landed, even if
we landed on a roof, in the sea.

Once, we followed winds that tasted of traffic
and rang sharp through the eaves.

So this is new, this choosing,
this watching ground,
then leaping,

hoping to be slowed by our samara,
hoping to land where we fall.

HIGHWAY 16, NEAR BLUE RIVER

Mountain highway, leg through skirts of spruce.
Recumbent, knee-capped.
We know this road. We're watching for the spot
where we hit the ditch that winter. Just to say, there.
There it is.
The road had awakened with a sudden kick
black ice flicked us like a fly.
If there'd been oncoming traffic—
if there'd been a stand of trees—
Now tourists park in the sun and run
across lanes to photograph elk.

Houseplants on the back seat
we're headed where the highway meets the ring road,
looking for home in the place it used to be.

                                          Here

after the bend.
No, the trees were thicker, no, the ditch was deeper.
If it had been at this cliff,
or there, the frozen lake—

But there was only snow. Now, thick brush
has grown over scars, it's summer
and the road is dry. We'll buy a little bungalow
and I'll sew curtains and you'll plant a garden.
We'll leave behind the winter, the glimpse,
the embankment, here
yes, the straight stretch where we waited
for the tow truck, snow filling our boots.

It may not really be the spot, and we don't stop anyway.
There's another line that marks the province
where in an instant we age an hour
and there's still miles to go.

TO VIOLET

who lived in this house before us, whose life
is alluded in flyer, offer, catalogue of seeds, I imagine
you ordered packets of yourself—Heart's Ease, Northern Bog
Viola sororia, Viola riviniana, blooms as song.
Though the colour's name comes from the flower
the flowers come too in yellow, blue, and white
and when we sleep inside these rooms we sleep
where you too slept and shat and swallowed. Your smoke
is in the walls, your flowers in the ground
Crowfoot, Long-Spurred, Common Dog
Return to sender, the seed, the glimpse, Violet
we're trying to grow something new—
They are perennial, these messages
of someone else's loss.

SPRING

Mittens lost in snow are budding in the grass
and now, it is still light after supper.
Maybe in a few months I will hold my belly
the way those women do —
saucer and cup,
palm full of birdseed.

This is the ice we loved as kids,
melt squishing under skin
like walking on the lens of an eye.
Maybe in a few years we'll follow
small boots across the frozen park,
remember when we too were light
and thought everything alive.

Now we wait for sky to hold its light
like water in a blue glass.
We put our scarves in our pockets
and there are so many birds.

SHOEBOX
PHOTOS

I.

There's Grandpa and his army buddies.
The same guys are in all these pictures.

They wear each other around their shoulders. Close
as their bunks, brined in sweat and bad breath,
the passed cigarette, lip damp.

> Remember the time we snuck into the garden
> and stole the carrots? The same night
> we got our tattoos, our maple leaves sore
> and all that beer.
> The lady yelling at us in German.

When the grave has been refilled with dirt, the remains
are these: the bachelor bed, neatly made,
the scrap wood ladder, cans of Prem,
and this shoebox genealogy.

The mother he could not remember, sepia pompadour.
The daughter he did, frozen in mary janes.
These uniformed boys

> pissing on the fence.
> And those German girls,
> I had never seen legs like those.

There are those you know: missing front teeth,
feathered bangs and Christmas card sweaters.
The family he loved when they came to mind.

When I told my grandchildren I was in Germany,
they thought I meant the War.

And those you don't know: black and white picket poses.
Ancestors interred in film, unmarked,
with handwritten pay stubs
and a recipe for pea soup cut from the paper.

We were just kids, then
playing tanks behind the school.

But there are things the box could hold
no more than water,

I still think of that when I eat them raw.
How the tops looked like green lace,
like the burlesque dancers.
How cocky we were.

pictures lost or taken
only with the mind.

That taste,
sweet and earth.

II.

This was one of Grandpa's brothers, and his daughters. Their mother
died. And that one, she spent her whole life in Ponoka.

The sheet hangs white and wide
beside their father, the studio
at a loss: How to compose
a family without a mother?

Both girls touch their faces,
hair clamped down like wash on the line.
Twitching in their dresses

> in our minds kicking
> off our shoes and socks,
> to pull a kite of twigs and paper.

> Last afternoon by the lake, when I called you
> "Sis," trying it out,
> something I had read in a book. *Sis.*

Why is it remarkable to spend your life
in that town, where the grain mirrors the sun,
and everyone waits all year for the rodeo?
All her life in Ponoka.

Then someone says, oh,
you mean the asylum.

> Chasing the kite, painted with a long broad beak.
> Dad told us a story
> of a girl who shrinks to the size of a pin
> and is swallowed by a bird.

And she is flying, far far away to Mexico.

You tell us she was one of those
sterilized by the government.
—But no, you don't say "sterilized."
Something like, they operated on her
so she could never have babies.
Without euphemism of cleanliness,
bleach and shiny metal in boiling water.

If we let go of the string
our bird will fly all the way to Mexico.
No, wait!

and the sky is white and wide
and the kite is drifting out over the lake
until it is the size of a pin.

Both girls touching their faces,
as if holding their jaws in place, holding
cheek flesh on bone.

Hey Sis, come on. Come on, Sis.

III.

Who is this?
No idea.

Her face is grey and her dress
may or may not be grey.

It was pink.

She doesn't think much
of her photographer, squinting
into sun or subjection. Hard
as the mountain in her wake,
cheeks slackened with scree,
angles where cartilage heaved
with hurts old as continents.

In the seam of her mouth
black dust, silent and cold
as coal unmined from its rock bed.

My name, now, is
only my own.

IV.

Is that a moose pulling a tractor?

I remember this photo. I asked him, Grandpa, what's this? He said,
it's a moose pulling a tractor.

V.

Who is that little girl in the blue dress? She's in a couple of these pictures.

Her face blurry
forgotten even by film.
Maybe a cousin

> That was always my favourite dress,
> blue the shade of that dragonfly
> we caught on the porch step.
> I told you it would bite
> so you would let me hold it

or maybe just a neighbour girl
caught in the shot,
fruit fly in a juice glass.

> *yeah,*
> *take a chunk out of your hand*
> *quick as a dog.*
> I thought I told a lie
> until it pinched me with its mandibles,
> that thin flesh between my forefinger and thumb.
> Your eyes wide with my bright wound.

> I saw, then, the power
> of my own words.
> To make a lie true,
> to draw blood.

Blond hair, messy with play,
a blue dress like a shallow pool
stained with raspberries.

                    Blood dripped, ruining my dress.
            But was it that same dress? That same afternoon?
                Or do I think it was only for the shade,
                        that same blue of the day,
                            of the dragonfly,
                        stained with all the things
                            I could make true.

DRINK
THE RIVER

MUSKEG

You had forgotten the smell of stars—
     cool and green,
     pine and quick rain.
But you fit here, telling me how muskeg doesn't freeze,
hazards before the road was paved.

Once you followed tracks through these woods,
looking for wolves
the kitchen light curtained by trees. You knew
your mother was drinking coffee at the table.

Home holds memories like nails in an ice cream pail.
This is where you raced dirtbikes, licking mud from your lips,
tobogganed on days too cold for school.

This is where you came after she died.
Home holds grief like leaves in an eavestrough,
water in the earth. Muskeg grief,
muddy grief that could suck
you down

but you know this country.
You know the taste of the ground.

IT NEVER RAINS

but it pours, my mother often said.
By which she meant appliances will break in threes,
a flu will follow the fender bender.

She didn't know rainforests aren't always jungles,
that there's a place west of Edson
where the air is verdant and the ground spongy with loss

where rain is not weather, but geography.

TWO PRINTS

There was an abandoned barn in the country
that your mother loved: rain-greyed, cleft
by Wildwood sky. Not because chic was shabby
milk crate picture frames and antiqued slates
with "Free Range Children." She was the woman
who heard life stories at every bus stop,
who sat in the kitchen with your friends
while they spilled heartache in their cups. The barn
had once seen foals shudder into the world,
stumble up on toothpick legs.

When you argued with your brother she heard two sides,
remembered you small, mewling for milk
and filled the breach like blue.
She died a year before I met you.
And I can only guess the shape of her loss.
She is a hole in you
the way your pupil is a hole in your eye.
But sometimes you tell me stories:

A young photographer she helped once
brought her two framed prints of her barn.
Picture what she loved: things lost or broken,
needing composition in good light.
Now one print hangs in your brother's house,
the other one in ours. Different angles
of the same rough planks, a hurt so deep
you're both sure it can't be shared.

Your brother does not remember
it was the wrong barn.

But this, to you, is the story. She smiled,
thanked her young photographer,
did not tell him his mistake. Instead she laughed
and hung them in the living room, quiet diptych, loved them
for the light through the roof's long apertures, loved them more
for their perfect fault.

ULTRASOUND

Two centuries ago they blindfolded bats
and saw they could still hunt.
Sound the shape of a thousand leaves.
I can't hear the trees within this night,

can't see in my own dark spaces.
Centuries ago they blindfolded bats, and saw
strange music, too high for human ears,
sound the shape of a thousand leaves.

The transducer pulses through gel and tissue.
I can't see in my own dark spaces,
mysteries of shape and shadow.
Strange music, too high for human ears

to hear. Instead it appears,
transducer pulsing through tissue,
reflections of my flesh
stippled as shape and shadow.

Twice before my body echoed
like a call into a drum.
The waves flow, ebb, become light
reflections of my flesh.

Pixels draw the spine of bass clef.
Twice before my body echoed.
Now a new pulse, drumming life.
The waves flow, ebb, become light.

Under water, whales and ships find reefs.
And I find you,
swimming in this half-moon harbour.
A new pulse, drumming life.

FOOD

Now it is me who is the egg
perched on a wall, afraid to sneeze.
And you, they say,

are a poppyseed.
I can taste you now, the way craving
is almost taste.

If I hold still long enough,
perhaps you'll stay
and in a few weeks more, become

a grape. They measure you in food
as if I swallowed you,
zygote on a spoon. As if

it is not me who is consumed.
You are a stain on my fingers,
scent on my breath,

so small a trace. Yet you
are already opium,
already wine.

RULES

Don't drink alcohol or smoke, of course.
No soft cheese, no processed meat or sushi.
No raw eggs: caesar salad dressing, runny benedicts.
Do not tell anyone till 12 weeks.
Don't exercise too hard, don't overheat.
Stay hydrated.
Avoid stress.
Remember you were made for this.
Visualize your uterus, thick with blood,
blooming around its fetal pole.
Do yoga, but not crow or upward facing dog.
No contact sports.
Hold your belly like glass.
Remember that loss is common, especially
in women who have lost before.
Check that your cervix is high and closed.
Check for blood.
Take folic acid. No Advil or cold medicine.
Sleep on your left side.
Visualize the blastocyst.
Read *Baby's Best Chance,*
keep it on your nightstand.
Avoid negative thoughts. Remember
that we all came from this, here
between hips sharp as knives.
Hold your belly
in your mind like a glass
of light. Hold it
upright.

NORTH SASKATCHEWAN

It carries glacial genes from the Icefields.
Snow fed, it knows
how to be a body in the cold.

Every day the train crossed the river,

     twenty seconds of light

between the tunnels through the banks.
I watched it freeze up,
     rafts of white snagging beneath the bridge,
          frazil ice,
        pans linked along the shoreline.
Inside me my son was building
white fat on bone.

He was born in December
when the days were narrowed,
seconds of light between the black banks
of a northern night.

Next December he will touch snow.
And watch the river from the bridge,
     the brushstrokes of wind,
     the city outfalls melting open leads.

Walleye and pike have learned
to live beneath the snow pack
to feed on cold minnows and darkness
that swim the silty channel bars.

And all year long we drink the river.

INCONGRUOUS

Sleeper with dump truck carrying
a basketball.
Washcloth with whale, anchor, sailboat
and squirrel.

My friend says, by way of congrats, Jen!
There's a *baby* in your house!

And you, lying on a blanket in your
dump truck-basketball sleeper, are breathing
like the Earth is young.

NURSE

First, it meant the woman not one's mother. Nutrix, or Old French nourrice
to feed the child too rich for milk of his own blood. Later, we must add "wet"
to get back to this meaning. As if the plump woman pulled
from her own brood by gilded tongue
had walked in rain, dripping to the crying lord.

A woman who cares for young children.
A woman who cares for the sick.

I felt your first fever in your hand, the small hot fingers at my neck
reassured by skin that held both, your milk and mother.
Could you taste my fear, let down like lead, dark issue
of motherhood? To wipe the sick from my shoulder
and fill you up again, slow,
praying you would keep it down. The noun came first,

then the verb. The being then the giving of her.
To cure, to care, to feed and to be fed
and to never have enough. To drink
slowly, from a single glass—

An infant's nose is short and flat so he can breathe here,
butterfly wing, falling feather, and fall asleep. Nourrice,
to nourish. To narrow fontanels, erupt teeth, lengthen limbs
beyond this need. But for now
your cheek shines with milk, and I am a serf
warmed by my own hearth.

FALLING BOUNDARY

in forestry: the boundary of an area marked for felling.
in linguistics: the intonation of a statement.

The stakes that hold the park's new saplings
are tied with neon orange logging tape
marked "falling boundary." Ribbon at a discount
or a bureaucrat's mistake, this is the whet edge of life

and lumber. My son grabs mulch from base of trunks
narrow as his arm. The stakes are sharp
but tape, toy-bright, flaps its invitation—
touch, pull. My son can't read, can't understand

that glass shards in the grass will cut
that sidewalk's edge is busy road
that there's a thousand ways one may be used. Falling boundary
also means the pitch of certainty at sentence end.

This is not a question. Don't trip, don't fall—
the stakes of this new growth.

"THE PERFECTION OF WOMANHOOD"

NATURAL CHILDBIRTH

coined by Grantly Dick-Read, obstetrician, 1933:

Woman

is adapted primarily for the perfection of womanhood

For millennia we have birthed the natural way

which is, according to the law of nature, reproduction.

For millennia we have birthed the natural way and we have suffered

and we have died for millennia we have been told the right way

to be a mother. *The art of natural childbirth has been lost*

except among women of more primitive types. You know what to do.

Healthy childbirth was never intended by natural law to be painful.

Hair cascades on pillow or pool, endorphins all the drug you need

as cervix softens like ripe fruit. *If left alone, just courage*

and patience are required. Was your birth natural was it normal

was it moral *influenced by natural emotions and perfected by the harmony*

of the mechanism.

Or did you stitch flesh together, animate the clay

with sparks? Natural is burrow, natural is tree sap drip, branch laden with apple

arsenic in the seed, blooms algaeic, aspergillum predator natural is maggot, rust

flood natural is holy natural is sacrifice. *Malaise or sickness seldom*

prevents [primitive women] from continuing such work

as they are in the habit of performing. Just breathe.

Your pain will empower you to be a real woman *No fears in her mind*

a real mother. *no knowledge of the tragedies of sepsis, infection*

and hemorrhage. Wouldn't you endure anything for your child?

To have conceived is her joy; the ultimate result of her conception

is her ambition. Tell me, yogi who has never birthed, tell me, Dick-

Read, that my pain is both my power and my fault.

Nothing will prepare me more for motherhood.

If left alone in labor, the body of a woman

produces most easily the baby that is not interfered with

by its mother's mind.

SON-OF-A-GUN

Early eighteenth century, origin unknown

but legend says that Navy-knocked-up women birthed
between broadside guns to keep the gangway clear. Origin
of accident, of fuck up. Cuss for toe-stub thumb-smash saying without saying
bitch. She laboured on rough blankets beneath barrels, waves
pushing her curse, monstrous spawn through flesh. Source
of raw deals, root of shafts. Woman must be to blame
for knife slip, bleach burn, limp cock, blood and mess
dropping lead to deck her screams lost in barrage. Son-of-a
suckles on canine teat, savage slap of tongue. We know
where this violent birth begins

EQUIVALENT

Governess, sovereign of sums and snot,
from governor; female equivalent.

Mistress, kept, as secret and stock
from master; female equivalent.

Courtesan, granted silk for skin,
from courtier; female equivalent.

Madam, damn them to the purchase,
the cocked john, from French for my lady;
see sir: female equivalent.

Hussy, head and hustle
from housewife, from sum and secret,
stock and damn, see head of household;
female equivalent.

BIKINI

It shook the earth. To see a woman's navel, flesh radiating in the glare. Twenty-three kilotons of Fat Man plutonium, the first test had turned Bikini's sky red days before. This was what Louis Réard wanted for his four triangles of cloth, the audacious progress, the blinding power. *For the good of mankind*

and to end all world wars they came with thousands of rats, goats, pigs. Came to force the islanders to a barren atoll. Nicknamed the first bomb Gilda, pasted it with Rita Hayworth's pic. Already said bombshell, ogled her curves. *It is not a bikini,*

Réard said, *unless it can be pulled through a wedding ring.* He said *it reveals everything about a girl except her mother's maiden name.* No professional model would wear it, so he hired a nude dancer from the Casino de Paris. Banned in Italy and Spain, women's bodies the limit of decency. On the beach

in Rongelap the Islanders saw two sunrises. Theirs is not my story to tell. But when I go swimming, the story sits unspoken on my body. How easily I slip it on, the triangles, the coconut SPF, the word that once meant home, printed with polka dots. Add the word bottoms, add the word wax, show my skin. It seems innocuous, now, the reposed navel

of the Bravo crater. But the crabs and coconut contain cesium-137. This is where a people lived. They wanted to know if the ships would sink, when the goats would die, they wanted to know how far they could push the limit. It reveals everything.

CONCESSION / STAND

I.

NOVEMBER 9, 2016

from Latin concedere, to give way

      Thank you. Thank you all. Soft
the drink, milk the dud. The peaceful transfer of Bounty, starburst.
Give way to pop, popcorn, butterfingers on All the women who put
their faith God bless you Good & plenty. I want you to know

    Today my infant daughter sat up. She is learning to
command her body, doesn't know yet that some think it and the
world are theirs, by right of white dick, drone and cluster

      Our constitutional democracy. Give
way, give away Suck it up, suck it back, the rage, the crush To all the
little girls Sweet tart Sugar baby I want you to know Some think
you and the world are on their tongues Make spheres of ice cream
call it progress Deep fry mars Deep throat whopper Make a wall
and cream it all Get your nuts Get your kicks You can do anything

        she says to
all the little girls and it could be true.

II.

ALBERTA, APRIL 16, 2019

There's a pattern in the vest spatter, ketchup-hued. A stick to the
floor from fountain popped through stolen land. Oh Alberta, yes
you are Strong. Screen muscle glowing in the dark, 3D punch and
music swells like pockets. Aisle strewn with tubs and cups—*Let's all
go to the lobby.* Call it butter but it's still oil.

(But my daughter, now, can sit, and stand
and raise her voice, and she is listening).

The earth rotates in heat lamp glow, but Ma'am, give way, for there's
a line, a show, a truck rumbling in. Give way to those who would
call genocide a Junior Mint. Whose idea of change is conversion of
the child. Who brand bumpers *Support the patch, let 'er idle.*

In this climate we are all idle
if we're not already on fire.

HOW THE RIVER CARVES OUR NAMES

MOTHER

mother, noun (1)

A woman who gives birth to a child.

from Middle English moder
from Old English modor
from Proto-Indo European mater

from baby-talk *ma,* the same in almost every language, every century. How the child who barely talks can name us, how the child who barely talks can make us. As in, Mama, come. As in, Mama I will take you everywhere, in follicles and fingernails.

As in, Mama, see the moon.

mother, noun (2)

A condition that gives rise to another. Of invention. Of pearl. Of all hangovers.
As in, you are the pixels and I am the picture. You are the matrix
and I am the flesh.

mother, verb (1)

To care for a child until adulthood. (*Compare* Father, *to fertilize the egg that conceives them*). To be both milk and cup. To feed, to bathe, to change, to watch, to clutch, to stretch, to shed, to hollow. To catch the cuff and pull it through to right-side-out. To fall in love while falling down the stairs. To picture flames, when you send them off to daycare so you can write—broken glass and possessions scattered on the road. To find snot in your own hair and hope banana. To read the story again, make toast as well as oatmeal. To be the bowl and table. To want to be the table. And to sometimes want to be the tree, reforested.

mother, noun (3)

The slimy membrane of yeast and bacteria that forms on the surface of
fermenting liquids. From Middle Dutch modder, *filth, dregs.*

Yelling at her dolls—is this how I sound to her? Digging in the plant
pots, fingers in her mouth. Beside me at the dinner table, ma-ma
baby talk, greasy face smashed into my shoulder. Wipe your face,
hands to yourself at supper, please. She only wants to hug, she only
wants to hold my arm so that my fork is suspended above my plate.
Mama I love you, staining me.

a thick substance concreting in liquors; the lees or scum concreted

dregs, lees: see Mud

mother, noun (3)

All moulds are inceptions of putrefaction; as the moulds of pies and flesh
abandoned pear sliming counter
                              and if the body be not apt to putrefy totally
it will cast up a mother   beneath the village eye
whose better judgment finds us prokaryotic. As in

that child should have a hat. That child's a little terror. Look
to the mother.   Compare the angel in the house, compare the vapour.
Raising voices don't raise children.   Fury at the fruit fly at the child
at the ideal ethereal-sleeved. Because she looms. Because

I want her to be possible. Look to the pear—
it will mould, if I leave it there. But I wanted them
to taste its sweetness.

The turbid sediment or lees which are formed in the course of fermentation, and seem to be the matrix from whence the pure product is sprung

From Proto-Indian-European mater,
also the source of matter,
as in the substance from which something is made. The clay, the raw.

as in, *Oh, dear, what can the matter be?* As in the reason for their tears. As in the one who left them. As in the one who is needed and the one who never has enough to give.

as in, *Oh, dear, what can the matter be? Johnny's so long at the fair.* As in the one who is left. She's chasing the fly, running through the field, forgetting fear, forgetting me, following iridescent wings.

as in, the matter is nothing
without the form.
The phonemes are nothing
without the story.

mother of all _____

As in the mother of all cities, the mother of all storms,
the mother of all sandwiches, all traffic jams, all bombs.
The phrase was brought to English when Saddam Hussein
called the Gulf War the mother of all battles.
As in pinnacle, climax, superlative, touching expletive and prayer
a way of saying everything at once

ONE LITTLE, TWO LITTLE, THREE LITTLE

bubbles. Our children are learning
how to count.
The pencil crayons are no longer Flesh
the reds are Apple and Flame
but this tune infests my head,
my son's, earworm,
parasite. Four little, five little, six little
verses, and it is not bubbles in the air—

we parents can hear them, still
sitting on rough carpets, itching
in our corduroy. But we can pretend
there is no violence in bubbles, no complicity in tunes, no pain
in swapped words. We can pretend we know the answers
like the names of all their body parts. Seven little eight little nine little
children, learning to count, learning their colours, learning
what it means to share.

LIONESS

Vertebrae and ears erect above the ridge,
black gum lick, then slip-stalking down the dune.
My son wants her to win, to confirm what he suspects:
that the world is made of need and violence.
The lioness must feed her cubs, or they will starve.
But the cubs are far behind in grass

and the lioness is running.
The music pounds to match her paws,
snout missiles through the heat.
Haunches hulk, then stretch, her flight
unhindered by the earth. This
is what she was built to do. I want her to win
for the beauty of her run
the grace of her need, the power
of her empty pounce.

She returns to her cubs, again
and again, jaws empty, golden hide
rib-furrowed. Teeth bared
but only as she catches her breath.

Slip the sleep in, the stop. The weight, the wave. Sound of crying. Sound of husband rising, murmur, water in the cup. Or sound of snoring and more crying, my own body lifting up the world. Blanket, nightlight, dream. *Can I sleep with you, can I sleep on the floor, can you sleep in my bed, can you stay for five minutes?* In the day, I see my own intelligence and creativity as if through frosted windshield, all sparkle and distortion, the taupe I know to be the house. Unknown toy clicking, but only till I try to find it. Numb click post check shop like and put the dishes on the other dishes, six years since I last slept through the night. Patience, then, a cat beneath the tire. Hello kitty, need to pee, peed the bed. Husband opening garage door at 2 a.m.—what are you doing? Back with the drill—*taking the blades off her ceiling fan. She's scared of the shadows.* I see the books I used to read, the books I used to write. Try to fit the laundry in the basket, couch lump numb click Awake to feeling of being watched. If I don't open my eyes. Tap tap tap on my shoulder, *I had a bad dream* Weight drop bed bounce breathing, still there. What was your dream about? *Um...monsters.* Scrape the window, scrape the dish Slip the stop, the snore, wave the click Cry the cup, taupe tire drill book floor years How much I want the thing I can't remember. What was your dream about?

PATIENCE

When mine is riddled with pox
splayed on table or slab
will you remind me patience
is from patientia, *quality of suffering?*

That it doesn't mean don't feel the ire, or cure it
but endure it
like a birth, expected tear
and unexpected haemorrhage

the red that runs in me, my child,
that makes both the fury and the love
the muddy floor, the muddy bank—tell me

abstract noun from patientem
supporting,
        bearing,
used of persons as well as navigable rivers

SEPTEMBER SNOW

When summer ends suddenly
I see you shimmering
as above a sun-baked road.
We have known heat.
We haven't yet deflated the kids' pool,
we haven't yet picked the herbs to dry
and your body glimpsed at bedtime between t-shirt and dark
is brown as the unchanged hares. The robins
look bewildered by the sugar covering their food.
They miss the earth
and if you should ever fall out of love with me
I, too, want to notice.

GO GREEN

Green, because the trees. Because the rainforest's canopy, light as long as history. Because the vine, the moss, the Honduran brook frog. But it could have easily been go blue. For clean sky, ocean swaddle. The whales. The rainy day, minor sax notes of loss. O don't let this love end. Can't go on livin' without you. Ten years, they say, to save our worlds. The ones that quiver on the surface of this sphere, the one of fingers sliding on guitar strings, of cotton sundress, white lines of novel spine, the one in which my daughter's hair is fine as dandelion spun to seed, and she turns on water just to make a rainbow in the spray. So go blue, go green, go kelly, go sage. Go green with envy of the ones still in denial. Go to the dark-veined forest. Go rogue, go feral. Because the fern, because the kakapo parrot. And when the sky is green from fire, go to the ends of Earth, with rinsed out soup cans and plastic made of corn. And if you don't believe that this is what it takes, let's find a way to mix the ocean with the sun.

PRECARIOUS

From the Latin precarius, held through the favour of another.

Once we snuck down to the slope below the trail, my skirt lifted to the canyon, your grip the only thing between my white flesh and the cactus. This was new enough, then, that I trusted love over gravity, desire over pain.

Not related, as one might think, to precipice. From the Latin, praecipitium, a steep place, from praeceps, headfirst. How the earth was loose against the bank, how everything that day was white with light.

We build a tower of blocks with our son, show him to make a strong base, show him balance. But everywhere there is colour, here a horse on a ledge, here an outcrop of blue. Here the head of an owl and the body of a fox. Could we make it tall as him, could we make it tall as us. And we can—now yellow, now red, this growing, wonderful thing. A place for us to live in the air. This defies physics—how we construct the floor as we stand upon it.

Not related, as one might feel, to precious. From Vulgar Latin precare, to ask earnestly, to beg. It is not the cliff to fear but the body you are holding, how firmly you grip it, how firmly it grips you. Not the cliff but the way the light is what can blind you.

Look how the river carves our names. Look how the hawk rides the heat. Look how high this thing we've built is.

From the Latin prex, entreaty, prayer.

If we fall from this great height, let it be that we were here, not in towers of our imagination. Let it be that we are part of the sky.

NOTES

The Frida Kahlo painting in "Gifts" is *Henry Ford Hospital, 1932*. The André Breton quote is originally from a 1938 brochure for an exhibition at the Julien Levy Gallery in New York.

Italicized lines in "Mother" are from Samuel Johnson, *A Dictionary of the English Language*, 1755; Francis Bacon, *Sylva Sylvarum*, 1626; and Hensleigh Wedgewood, *A Dictionary of English Etymology*, 1872. The phrase "Mother of all battles" is from a famous 1991 speech by Sadam Hussein, translated by Associated Press, https://apnews.com/article/c79824a72471a23f1adbf65cfc9627bf.

Italicized lines in "Natural Childbirth" are from Grantly Dick-Read, *Natural Childbirth* (1933); Childbirth Without Fear, London: Pollinger, 2006, originally published in 1942 as *Revelations of Childbirth*; and a 1958 unpublished manuscript, quoted in Donald Caton, "Who Said Childbirth Is Natural?: The Medical Mission of Grantly Dick Read," *Anesthesiology*, 1996.

In "Bikini," the phrase "for the good of mankind and to end all wars" was used by US Navy Commodore Ben H. Wyatt in an address to the Bikini Islanders in 1946.

Some phrases in "Concession / Stand" Part I are taken from Hilary Clinton's 2016 concession speech, https://www.theguardian.com/us-news/2016/nov/09/hillary-clintonconcession-speech-full-transcript. Part II was written in response to Rachel Notley's defeat in the 2019 Alberta provincial election to Jason Kenney's United Conservative Party.

Many sources were consulted in the research for this project; the *Online Etymology Dictionary* at etymonline.com was a particularly valuable resource. The line *"used of persons as well as navigable rivers"* in "Patience" is from this source.

ACKNOWLEDGMENTS

This book was written in Amiskwaciwâskahikan/Edmonton/ Treaty 6 territory, a home and gathering place of diverse Indigenous peoples including the Cree, Blackfoot, Métis, Nakota Sioux, Iroquois, Dene, Ojibway/Saulteaux/Anishinaabe, Inuit, and many others; and in Vancouver on the unceded territory of the Musqueam, Squamish and Tsleil-Waututh First Nations. As a settler, this context continually informs my writing and my desire to learn. I am honoured to create in these places, and aspire to do so with respect, humility and gratitude.

Thanks to the many readers who provided generous feedback, particularly Jannie Edwards, Claire Kelly, and Wendy McGrath.

Thanks to the editors who published earlier versions of:

"September Snow" in *The Compressed Journal of Literary Arts* (Jan. 2020).
"Muskeg" in *Funicular 3* (2019).
"Vancouver" in *Prairie Fire 36.3* (2013).
"North Saskatchewan" in *The 40 Below Anthology Vol. 2*. Ed. Jason Lee Norman. Wufniks Press (2015).
"Anemochory" in *Contemporary Verse 2* (Spring 2015).
"Know the Way" in *Arc* (Winter 2015).
"Gravity" and "Instinct" in *The Nashwaak Review 28/29* (2012).
"February in Vancouver" in *The Prairie Journal 58* (2012).
"The Way We Stand" in *dandelion 32.2* (2016).

Thanks to Shelly Donkin for some of the inspiration behind "Shoebox Photos."

Thanks, finally, to my family, for letting me write about them, and for the love and support.

Other Titles from University of Alberta Press

THE BAD WIFE

MICHELINE MAYLOR

An intimate, first-hand account of how to ruin a marriage.

Robert Kroetsch Series

GOSPEL DRUNK

AIDAN CHAFE

A poet's struggle for identity and salvation in the face of religious dogma and alcoholism.

Robert Kroetsch Series

FIELDS OF LIGHT AND STONE

ANGELINE SCHELLENBERG

Memory and reality, homeland and settlement, life and death—uncovering sacrifices, secrets, and forgiveness.

Robert Kroetsch Series

More information at uap.ualberta.ca